CONTENTS

THE WORLD CUP   4

BRAZIL 1958   6

ENGLAND 1966   8

BRAZIL 1970   10

NETHERLANDS 1974   12

WEST GERMANY 1974   14

ARGENTINA 1986   16

FRANCE 1998   18

ITALY 2006   20

SPAIN 2010   22

GERMANY 2014   24

AGAINST THE ODDS   26

WORLD CUP EXPERT QUIZ   28

GLOSSARY, WORLD CUP WINNERS TABLE & FURTHER INFORMATION   30

INDEX   32

THE WORLD CUP

The World Cup is a month-long celebration of football which is held every four years. Teams from 32 countries battle it out on the pitch for the ultimate prize in football – the World Cup trophy.

WHAT MAKES A GREAT TEAM?

Firstly it doesn't have to be a team that has won the World Cup. The Netherlands were beaten finalists, but so captured people's imagination that they have never been forgotten.

PICKING THE BEST

This book has tried to include only one team for each national side, the exception being Brazil and Germany. Otherwise teams such as Italy and Argentina might have had more than one inclusion. The great Brazil sides of 1958 and 1970 have been picked above the teams of 1962, 1994 and 2002, though all were fine sides.

CLASS ACTS

What qualities should a great team have? Sometimes it is simply brilliant players and the scoring of wonderful goals such as Brazil in 1958 and 1970, or possessing a genius who inspires lesser players, as was the case with Maradona's Argentina in 1986. Or it might lie in a quality team packed with talent such as France in 1998 or with a brilliant short-passing game such as Spain produced in 2010.

WORLD CUP FAST FACTS

FOUNDED: 1930

NUMBER OF TEAMS THAT TAKE PART: 32 (expanded to 16 in 1934, 24 in 1982, and 32 in 1998)

MOST SUCCESSFUL TEAM: Brazil

TOP GOAL-SCORER: Miroslav Klose with 16

FORMAT: For the group stage, teams are put in eight groups of four teams. Each team plays all the other three teams once. The top two teams from each group qualify for the knockout stages, where the winner of one group plays the runner-up of another. The winners of this qualify for the eight-team quarter-finals, which are followed by the semi-finals and the long-awaited World Cup final itself.

...BALL
...RT
...CIAL
...OF
...P...
...TEAMS

Pete May

W
FRANKLIN WATTS
LONDON • SYDNEY

Franklin Watts
Published in Great Britain in 2017 by The Watts Publishing Group

Series Editor: Julia Bird
Series Design: d-r-ink.com

Picture credits: AFP/Getty Images: 14, 17c. AGIF/Shutterstock: 24. Allsport/Hulton Archive/Getty Images: 9b. The Asahi Shimbun/Getty Images: 1, 21. Bongarts/Getty Images: 17b, 27t. Lutz Bongarts/Getty Images: 19t. Shaun Botterill/Getty Images: 27b. Gabriel Bouys/AFP/Getty Images: 22t. Philippe Caron/Sygma Corbis/Getty Images: 18-19. Corbis Wire/Getty Images:13. dpa/Corbis/Getty Images: 9t, 15. Freepik.com: front cover c. fstockphoto/Shutterstock: 5t. Getty Images: 5b. Keystone/Hulton Archive/Getty Images: 8. Michael King/Getty Images: 16. Jessica F Moore/istockphoto: front cover t. Popperfoto/Getty Images: 7, 10, 11, 28. Christophe Simon/AFP/Getty Images: 23. Bob Thomas/Getty Images: 4r, 12, 20, 26, 29. Philippe Le Telier/Paris Match/Getty Images: 7. Richard Wareham /Fotografie Alamy: 25.

Dewey number: 796.3'34668
ISBN 978 1 4451 6127 3

Printed in China

Franklin Watts
An imprint of
Hachette Children's Group
Part of The Watts Publishing Group
Carmelite House
50 Victoria Embankment
London EC4Y 0DZ

An Hachette UK Company
www.hachette.co.uk
www.franklinwatts.co.uk

MIX
Paper from responsible sources
FSC® C104740

Spain take on Honduras during a group match in the 2010 World Cup.

CHARACTER AND TEAM SPIRIT

But greatness can also lie in having the character to overcome adversity, as was the case with the Italy side of 2006. It can also mean possessing the mental strength and determination to overcome an early goal and a supposedly better team, as West Germany proved by beating the Netherlands in 1974. In other cases it might simply be where the team is a perfect fit and becomes more than the sum of its parts, as was the case with England in 1966.

Any choice of top ten World Cup teams will always be open to argument, and we hope that this book will inspire many discussions. But hopefully the reader will agree that these teams all deserve to be included.

England players celebrate Hurst's controversial goal against West Germany in the 1966 World Cup.

Pelé brought new skill and flair to the World Cup.

BRAZIL 1958

FAST FACTS

KIT: Yellow shirts with green trim, blue shorts, white socks with yellow and green trim. Wore blue-shirted away strip in the final

MANAGER: Vicente Feola

CAPTAIN: Hilderaldo Bellini

KEY PLAYER: Pelé, the 17-year-old boy who stunned the world with his skill and maturity

BEST PERFORMANCE: Scoring five goals in the final against Sweden, the host side

In 1958 the 17-year-old Pelé lit up the World Cup tournament. The world had seen nothing like the young genius from Brazil who scored a hat-trick in the semi-final and two goals in the World Cup final.

TALENTED TEAM

But manager Vicente Feola had an array of talent in his squad and also selected another youngster, Garrincha, a wonderfully skilful right winger who had been born with bent legs (his left leg curved outward and his right leg inward). He could fool defenders by twisting and turning in unusual directions. Vavá was a lethal striker, who also scored twice in the semi-final and final, while midfielder Didi was a great passer and free kick specialist.

TIME TO SHINE

In the group games Brazil beat Austria 3–0 and were held to a goalless draw by England. Pelé was only selected for Brazil's final group game, a 2–0 win against the Soviet Union thanks to two Vavá goals, but then took the tournament by storm. In the quarter-final Pelé scored the only goal against Wales, a chest trap and turn followed by a fine finish. In the semi-final he scored a sensational hat-trick as Brazil thrashed France 5–2.

FINAL GLORY

The final was a tense game for Brazil, playing the host side Sweden in front of a home crowd. Brazil was still haunted by the way their side had lost the 1950 World Cup final 2–1 at home to Uruguay, despite taking the lead. When Sweden scored after four minutes through Liedholm it looked like disaster might occur again. But Garrincha set up two goals for Vavá to put Brazil ahead at half-time. Then Pelé produced a brilliant third, flicking the ball over the head of a defender and turning to volley home. Zagallo added a fourth, before the Swedes pulled a goal back, but then Pelé headed a fifth goal in injury-time. The 17-year-old was in tears of happiness at the final whistle before Brazil paraded the Swedish flag on their lap of honour. This great Brazil side had won the World Cup for the first time and Pelé was on his way to becoming a global superstar.

DID YOU KNOW?

Garrincha also starred in the 1962 World Cup side and was one of the first footballers to have a pop star girlfriend in samba singer, Elza Soares, whom he married in 1966.

Brazil celebrate winning the 1958 World Cup with a joyful lap of honour.

ENGLAND
1966

'Some people are on the pitch... they think it's all over... it is now!' Geoff Hurst's fourth goal for England, accompanied by Kenneth Wolstenholme's commentary, provided English football with its greatest moment. Hurst scored a hat-trick as West Germany were beaten 4–2 in the 1966 World Cup final at Wembley.

FAST FACTS

KIT: White shirts, navy blue shorts, white socks. Famously changed to second kit of red shirts white shorts and red socks for the final

MANAGER: Sir Alf Ramsey

CAPTAIN: Bobby Moore

KEY PLAYER: Geoff Hurst, who replaced Jimmy Greaves and scored a hat-trick in the final

BEST PERFORMANCE: Recovering from the disappointment of a late German equaliser to score twice in extra-time in the final

NEW FORMATION

England won the World Cup through the tactical awareness of manager Sir Alf Ramsey. His team used a new 4-4-2 formation, relying on hard-working midfielders rather than wingers. England had world-class players in goalkeeper Gordon Banks, defender Bobby Moore and midfielder Bobby Charlton who was famed for his long-range shooting. Martin Peters was good at drifting into space and Alan Ball never stopped working.

GROWING CONFIDENCE

In the group matches England started nervously in a goalless draw with Uruguay, but then defeated Mexico 2-0 with goals from Roger Hunt and a Bobby Charlton rocket. They went on to beat France 2-0 and defeated Argentina 1-0 in the quarter-final after the Argentine captain Rattin was sent off for dissent in a bad-tempered clash. In the semi-final England beat Portugal 2-1. Stiles marked Portugal's star man Eusebio out of the game and Bobby Charlton scored twice, the second with a typically strong shot.

Sir Alf Ramsey

DISASTER STRIKES

Ramsey preferred the hard-working Hurst to crowd favourite Greaves in the World Cup final. Germany took the lead through Haller after just 12 minutes. But England equalised through Hurst's header and then took the lead when Peters pounced on a rebound after 78 minutes. It looked like England's cup until two minutes from the end when Weber bundled the ball home as England claimed for an earlier handball. As the players waited for extra-time Ramsey showed his motivational skills, telling his men: 'Look at the Germans, they're flat out... You've won the World Cup once, now go out and win it again.'

TIME FOR HEROES

England responded. Hurst controlled Ball's cross, turned and shot against the bar. The ball bounced on the goal line as Roger Hunt appealed for a goal. After consulting the linesman the referee gave the goal. It would have been a controversial winner, but in the final moments Moore remained the calmest man on the pitch as he played a great long pass from defence to Hurst, who burst through the tired German defence to hammer the ball into the top of the net. England had won the World Cup for the first and only time.

Hurst heads home to equalise the game at 1-1.

DID YOU KNOW?

The World Cup was stolen before the 1966 World Cup Finals. After seven days it was found in some south London bushes by a dog called Pickles.

England parade the World Cup in front of an ecstatic home crowd.

BRAZIL 1970

Brazil's 1970 World Cup winners were possibly the greatest side ever to play international football. This World Cup was the first to be shown on colour TV and the bright yellow, green and blue kit of Brazil seemed to perfectly match their so-called 'samba football'.

DID YOU KNOW?

Pelé is the only player to have three World Cup winners medals – for 1958, 1962 (he was awarded a medal later even though he was injured for the later games) and 1970.

Brazil's Tostão and Pelé celebrate a typically stylish Brazilian goal.

FAST FACTS

KIT: Yellow shirts with green trim, blue shorts, white socks with green and yellow trim

MANAGER: Mário Zagallo

CAPTAIN: Carlos Alberto

KEY PLAYER: Gerson, whose passing orchestrated the brilliant forward line

BEST PERFORMANCE: Demolishing Italy 4–1 in the World Cup final

The Brazilian and Italian teams line up before the 1970 final.

TEAM BRAZIL

Just as in 1958, the brilliant Pelé was the star of the team, scoring four goals during the tournament. However, manager Mario Zagallo could also call upon the explosive left-foot shooting of Rivelino and the brilliant dribbling and finishing of Jairzinho, who scored in all six World Cup games. Striker Tostão was an able partner for Pelé up front, while midfielder Gerson was a great passer who set the pace of the team.

UPS AND DOWNS

Brazil's defensive lapses only added to the entertainment, as they beat Czechoslovakia 4–1 and Romania 3–2 in group games. Their match against England was a much tougher game, won 1–0 through Tostão's cross, Pelé's lay-off and Jairzinho's great finish. Peru were beaten 4–2 in the quarter-final. In the semi-final, Brazil were a goal down to old rivals Uruguay but responded with a brilliant finish from Clodoaldo and late efforts from Jairzinho and Rivelino to win the game 3–1 and reach the World Cup final once again.

SAMBA GLORY

The final itself was a great display of attacking football against a defensive Italian side. Pele scored a header to put Brazil ahead, only for a defensive lapse to let Boninsegna score an equaliser. Gerson scored the second with a thumping shot. Jairzinho poked home the third before captain Carlos Alberto overlapped to score possibly the greatest team goal in World Cup history. An eight-man passing move included midfielder Clodoaldo beating four men in his own half, and ended with Rivelino and Jairzinho setting up Pelé's pass and Alberto's superb drive into the bottom corner. The world could only sit back and admire the boys from Brazil.

NETHERLANDS 1974

Playing in brilliant orange shirts, the Netherlands side lit up the 1974 World Cup with 'total football', a term invented by the Dutch press after the 4–1 demolition of Bulgaria in the group stage. Rinus Michels' side had players constantly changing positions, a new tactic which baffled the opposition.

FAST FACTS

KIT: Orange shirts with black arm stripes, white shorts with orange stripes at sides, orange socks with black trim

MANAGER: Rinus Michels

CAPTAIN: Johan Cruyff

KEY PLAYER: Johan Cruyff, whose genius illuminated the World Cup

BEST PERFORMANCE: Beating Brazil 2–0 in the final group game

Johan Neeskens (left) and Johnny Rep of the Netherlands.

Neeskens sends the German goalkeeper the wrong way to score for the Netherlands.

TEAM EFFORT

Johan Cruyff was the star man, a superb dribbler, goal maker and taker. He gave his name to the 'Cruyff turn', after a feint and drag back move that baffled Sweden's right back Jan Olsson. Johan Neeskens was a skilful midfielder, while Johnny Rep was an exciting striker who netted four times. In defence, Arie Haan was a strong centre back and Ruud Krol an attacking left back who could also score goals.

TOTALLY AMAZING

The genius of the Dutch side was seen in the second round as they defeated Argentina 4–0. Every goal was pure class; Cruyff's instant control as he rounded the keeper for the first, Krol's blast from the edge of the area, Cruyff's cross for a flying Rep header and then Cruyff scoring from a seemingly impossible angle. A 2–0 victory over East Germany was followed by the crucial 2–0 defeat of a strong Brazil side in the decisive group game. Neeskens scored with a volley from Cruyff's cross. Then the Dutch produced a classic team goal, breaking from their own area with Krol's cross being met by Cruyff's flying volley. The Dutch would face West Germany in the World Cup final in Munich.

FINAL PAIN

If anything the Netherlands started the final too well, with a 14-man passing move ending with Cruyff being brought down in the area. Neeskens converted the penalty after just two minutes before the Germans had even touched the ball. But they reckoned without German spirit and the support for the home team. Breitner equalised with a disputed penalty and Gerd Müller grabbed a goal just before half-time. Despite several chances in the second half, the Dutch failed to equalise. But with their total football, Adidas-sponsored kit and cool sideburns, the Dutch side remains arguably the greatest team not to win the World Cup.

DID YOU KNOW?

While the rest of the Dutch side had three black stripes on their sleeves representing sponsors Adidas, Cruyff played with just two stripes as he was sponsored by rivals Puma.

WEST GERMANY 1974

The West Germany side that won the World Cup in 1974 is often underrated simply because they beat the people's favourites, the Johan Cruyff-inspired Netherlands. But having the character to recover from conceding a second-minute penalty proved the West Germans' heart and class.

West German defender Berti Vogts (right) tackles Australian forward Branko Buljevic during the group game between West Germany and Australia.

FINE FINISHERS

West Germany possessed a truly world-class striker in Gerd Müller. 'Der Bomber' scored a total of 14 goals in the 1970 and 1974 World Cups. The side also had the great Franz Beckenbauer at the back, a sweeper as good coming forward as he was defending. Wolfgang Overath was a fine playmaker and Sepp Maier a superb goalkeeper. In Paul Breitner they had an overlapping left back with a great shot.

WINNING WAYS

West Germany beat Chile and Australia in their group matches. Ironically the only match they lost was a 1–0 defeat to East Germany. In the second round West Germany beat Yugoslavia 2–0, with a great 35-yard strike from Breitner and a snatched goal from Müller. They scored four times in the second half against Sweden and, in a vital last game on a soggy pitch, beat a fine Poland side 1–0 with a confident finish from Müller. Manager Helmut Schön stood arms aloft on the touchline as the Germans reached the World Cup final.

AGAINST THE ODDS

In the final the Dutch scored with a penalty before a West German player had touched the ball. It was a huge blow in front of a loud home crowd, but slowly the West Germans played themselves back into the game. Breitner scored a disputed penalty and the West Germans played their own brand of total football with defenders Beckenbauer and Vogts going close to scoring. Just before half-time Gerd Müller scored with a fantastic finish, somehow spinning to hook home Bonhof's cross with the ball behind him. Sepp Maier had a great game in the second half as an inspired Berti Vogts marked Cruyff out of the game. The Dutch might have been in brilliant orange compared to West Germany's white and black, but the mental strength and footballing ability of the West Germans deserved the ultimate prize.

West German players celebrate their second goal against the Netherlands.

FAST FACTS

KIT: White shirts with black trim, black shorts, white socks

MANAGER: Helmut Schön

CAPTAIN: Franz Beckenbauer

KEY PLAYER: Gerd Müller might not have looked like a typical striker, but he had a great goalscoring instinct

BEST PERFORMANCE: Overcoming the blow of an early penalty to beat the total football of the Dutch

ARGENTINA
1986

The genius of Diego Maradona means it is often overlooked that the Argentina side that won the 1986 World Cup in Mexico had ten other good players.

SPIRITED SIDE

Defender José Luis Brown, who scored his only goal for Argentina in the World Cup final and then refused to be substituted despite having a dislocated shoulder, sums up the spirit of the side. Jorge Valdano was a fine attacking midfielder who scored four goals in the tournament, while Oscar Ruggeri was a talented defender. Though Maradona was the undoubted star of the team, Argentina's manager Carlos Bilardo deserves much credit for his handling of Maradona, making him feel special by appointing him captain and building a team around his talents. He was rewarded with performances of genius.

BEST AND WORST

In the group stage, Argentina beat both South Korea and Bulgaria and drew 1–1 with Italy thanks to Maradona's equaliser. In the quarter-final against England, Maradona scored the infamous 'Hand of God' goal with his hand, but then produced the 'goal of the century', dribbling from his own half to beat five defenders and score. He then scored a brilliant double in the semi-final win against Belgium.

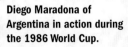

Diego Maradona of Argentina in action during the 1986 World Cup.

FANTASTIC FINAL

The final against West Germany was a thriller. Despite Maradona being man-marked at every turn, Argentina went 2–0 up through Brown's header and Valdano's fine finish after 56 minutes. But West Germany once more showed all their fighting spirit to score twice and level the game after 81 minutes through Rudi Völler. Three minutes later Maradona received the ball just inside his own half and released Jorge Burruchaga with a superb pass. The striker kept his nerve during a 40-yard run to slot the ball past Germany's Schumacher. Argentina held on, and ticker tape rained down from the stands as Maradona lifted the World Cup.

FAST FACTS

KIT: Light blue and white striped shirts, black shorts, white socks

MANAGER: Carlos Bilardo

CAPTAIN: Maradona

KEY PLAYER: Maradona, who could turn a match with one moment of genius

BEST PERFORMANCE: Beating West Germany 3–2 in the final having lost a two-goal lead

DID YOU KNOW?

Substitute Marcelo Trobbiani came on for the last two minutes of the final, equalling the record for the shortest ever World Cup career!

Burruchaga slides home Argentina's third and decisive goal.

FRANCE 1998

France's finest ever side was full of talent and character. They combined to take France to World Cup glory in 1998 for the first and only time in its history.

PACKED WITH TALENT

In goal was the dramatic, shaven-headed Fabian Barthez, a great shot-stopper. The defence had excellent full-backs in Thuram and Lizarazu, the giant Marcel Desailly and the classy Laurent Blanc. Les Bleus had a brilliant midfield with the underrated Didier Deschamps shielding the defence, a number of creative players like Emmanuel Petit, Christian Karembeu and Youri Djorkaeff, and the genius of Zinedine Zidane supporting lone striker Guivarc'h.

GOLDEN GOALS

As the home side at the 1998 World Cup, France finally played to their potential. Manager Aimé Jacquet's men beat South Africa, Saudi Arabia and Denmark in the group stages with a young Thierry Henry scoring three times. France had to rely on an extra-time 'golden goal' (the first team to score in extra-time won the match, an idea that was later scrapped) from Laurent Blanc to defeat Paraguay in the knockout match, before defeating Italy on penalties in the quarter-finals.

LATE DRAMA

The French showed character in the semi-final against Croatia, having fallen behind to a Davor Šuker goal.

Defender Lilian Thuram picked the perfect time to score his first ever international goal and then, amazingly, added a second, winning a tackle on the edge of the area and firing home with a perfect left-foot finish. Barthez made a crucial late tip-over save to see the French through to the final. The match was marred by Croatia's Slaven Bilić going down as if hit in the face after a tussle with Blanc. Blanc was sent off and missed the final through suspension.

WORLD CUP HISTORY

France met Brazil in the final at the Stade de France in Paris. Brazil's star striker Ronaldo had a fit on the eve of the match, and though selected, he did not appear fit to play. France took full advantage. Zinedine Zidane scored twice with powerful headers from corners to leave France 2-0 up at half-time. Les Bleus survived Desailly being sent off after collecting a second yellow card, and in the 90th minute, substitute Patrick Vieira released his Arsenal teammate Emmanuel Petit, who scored a third goal to send France into ecstasy. The suspended Blanc joined in the celebrations as captain Didier Deschamps proudly lifted the World Cup trophy.

FAST FACTS

KIT: Blue shirts with white arm stripes and red and white lines on chest, white shorts, red socks

MANAGER: Aimé Jacquet

CAPTAIN: Didier Deschamps

KEY PLAYER: Zinedine Zidane, who could find space anywhere on the pitch and scored twice in the World Cup final

BEST PERFORMANCE: Outplaying Brazil in the final and winning 3–0

French striker Thierry Henry takes the ball past Abdullah Zubromawi of Saudi Arabia.

France's players savour World Cup triumph at last.

DID YOU KNOW?

Goalkeeper Fabien Barthez insisted on a good luck kiss on his shaven head from teammate Lauren Blanc before every World Cup game.

ITALY 2006

The Italian side of 2006 proved its greatness through showing character in adversity. Following a corruption scandal in the Italian league, many of the Azzurri players were unsure if their teams would be relegated or where they would even be playing the following season.

FAST FACTS

KIT: Blue shirts, blue shorts, blue socks

MANAGER: Marcello Lippi

CAPTAIN: Fabio Cannavaro

KEY PLAYER: Goalkeeper Gianluigi Buffon, who made a crucial save to deny Zidane the winning goal in the World Cup final

BEST PERFORMANCE: Beating Germany in the semi-final with two goals in the final two minutes of extra-time.

DID YOU KNOW?

Ten different players scored for Italy in the tournament and five out of 12 goals were scored by substitutes, showing what a great team effort it was.

USA striker Carlos Bocanegra leaps high to head the ball against Italy in their group tie.

ENERGY AND RESOLVE

Goalkeeper Gianluigi Buffon had opted to stay with his team Juventus, relegated to the second division. He was outstanding in the World Cup, conceding just two goals. Centre back and captain Cannavaro was one of the players of the tournament. The energy of Gennaro Gatusso in midfield summed up the Italian spirit, while playmaker Andrea Pirlo provided the class. Italy topped their group with two wins and a draw, but in the knockout stages had to wait for a 95th minute penalty to beat a plucky Australian side, before defeating Ukraine 3–0 in the quarter-final, with Luca Toni scoring twice.

GREAT GAME

In the semi-final Italy defeated an impressive German side 2–0 after extra-time. It was a fast, exciting match. Buffon had already made a superb save from Podolski in extra-time and as a penalty shoot-out loomed, the Italians scored twice in the final two minutes. After 119 minutes Fabio Grosso scored with a curling shot, having been found by a fine reverse pass from Pirlo. As Germany pressed, Cannavaro intercepted and

found Gilardino who broke and rolled the ball to Del Piero, who curled home another delicate finish.

LATE DRAMA

In the World Cup final in Berlin, many expected veteran Zinedine Zidane to inspire France to victory. Zidane chipped in a penalty after seven minutes, but again the Italians refused to lie down. Giant centre back Materazzi equalised after 19 minutes with a header and the final went into extra-time. The crucial incident came in the first period of extra-time when Buffon produced a brilliant save to tip over Zidane's header. This seemed to unnerve Zidane so much that after an argument with Materazzi a few minutes later, he inexplicably headbutted him and was sent off.

BRAVE BLUES

The final finished 1–1 in normal time, but Italy kept their nerve to win 5–3 on penalties. The deciding penalty was struck by Grosso, who was jumped on by his ecstatic teammates. The squad had every excuse to fail, but instead brought glory to the troubled world of Italian football.

Italy captain and talisman Cannavaro proudly holds aloft the World Cup trophy.

'Tiki taka' champions of the world – Spain rejoice in their World Cup success.

FAST FACTS

KIT: Red shirts, blue shorts, red socks. Won the final in away kit of all navy blue with red and gold stripes

MANAGER: Vicente Del Bosque

CAPTAIN: Iker Casillas

KEY PLAYER: Andrés Iniesta was at the heart of Spain's 'tiki taka' system

BEST PERFORMANCE: Overcoming a resilient and skilful German side in the semi-final through Puyol's header

SPAIN 2010

This Spain side was renowned for its 'tiki taka' short passing game. The heartbeat of the side was provided by Barcelona midfielders Andrés Iniesta and Xavi, with the pair enjoying a great understanding.

BEST TEAM EVER?

Every player in Vicente Del Bosque's side was technically gifted, from centre back Gerard Piqué to superb passer Xabi Alonso and brilliant finisher David Villa. The Spaniards had the experience of Iker Casillas in goal, Sergio Busquets holding the midfield, a classy right back in Sergio Ramos and a battle-hardened defender in rugged Carlos Puyol. Players as gifted as David Silva, Cesc Fabregas and Fernando Torres could not even get into the starting eleven.

GETTING THROUGH

Spain might not have thrashed any sides in South Africa, but they always did enough to win, overcoming a shock first-game defeat to Switzerland. Portugal were beaten by a David Villa goal in the knockout match, while in the quarter-final against Paraguay both sides had a penalty saved before Villa again put Spain through with his fifth goal of the tournament. The mark of a great side is that they can win games through unexpected means. Spain did that against Germany in the semi-final, scoring an unusually direct goal as Puyol rose to meet Xavi's corner and thump a header into the net.

FIERY FINALE

The final against the Netherlands in Johannesburg was an bad-tempered game, full of strong tackles and with few chances. Dutch defender Heitinga was sent off in extra-time and the game was goalless until Jesus Navas burst into the Dutch half and started a passing movement that resulted in the ball rebounding off a defender to Fabregas. He found Iniesta with a short pass and the little midfielder drove the bouncing ball into the corner of the net. The goal sparked delirium as Iniesta ran to the corner and revealed a white vest with a tribute to the late Dani Jarque, a former youth player who died in 2009, before disappearing into a mass of teammates and substitutes. That moment showed the togetherness of the Spain squad as a nation rejoiced at winning its first World Cup trophy.

DID YOU KNOW?

Iker Casillas became the third goalkeeping captain to lift the World Cup, following the example of two Italians, Gianpiero Combi in 1934 and Dino Zoff in 1982.

Rugged Spanish defender Carlos Puyol heads the only goal of the game in the 2010 World Cup semi-final against Germany.

2014 FIFA World Cup™ Champ

GERMANY
2014

The 2014 World Cup saw a footballing giant reawaken as Germany won their fourth World Cup, their first since 1990. This formidable German team became the first European team to win a World Cup in North or South America.

DID YOU KNOW?

Germany's 7-1 defeat of Brazil was the worse loss ever suffered by a host nation and broke Brazil's 62-match unbeaten streak at home that dated back to 1975!

A SOLID TEAM

The Germans had a high-class team from back to front. Number one Manuel Neuer was undoubtedly the best goalkeeper in the world. Centre back Jérôme Boateng was solid as a rock in defence alongside the captain and rampaging right back Philipp Lahm. The midfield oozed class with the passing machine Toni Kroos and the creative genius of Mesut Özil. Up front Germany had the prolific Thomas Müller who scored five goals in the tournament and one of the top scorers in World Cup history Miroslav Klose.

ADVANCE TO THE SEMIS

Germany topped their group including a thumping 4-0 victory over their most dangerous opponents Portugal. Müller bagged himself a hat-trick. In the knockout stages Germany squeezed past Algeria 2-1 in extra time, and edged France 1-0 in the quarter-finals with an early goal from defender Mats Hummels who headed in a whipped free kick from Kroos. This set up a mouth-watering semi-final against the hosts and tournament favourites Brazil.

The German team line up to celebrate winning the World Cup.

FAST FACTS

KIT: White shirts with red chevron and black arm stripes, white shorts with red trim and black side stripes, white socks with red and black trim

MANAGER: Joachim Löw

CAPTAIN: Philipp Lahm

KEY PLAYER: Toni Kroos who scored twice and made four assists (the joint highest at the tournament)

BEST PERFORMANCE: Humiliating hosts Brazil 7-1 in the semi-final 8–3 in a group game

DEMOLITION JOB

The semi-final was nothing short of stunning. Within the first half an hour Germany were 5-0 up and had scored four of the goals in the space of six minutes. Some of the home crowd were so shocked that they were reduced to tears. Germany's second goal was scored by Klose which saw him become the all-time leading World Cup scorer with 16. By the final whistle the score was 7-1!

THE CLIMAX

In the final Germany faced old foes Argentina. After their semi-final rout the Germans showed a different side to their game. The resolute defence kept Argentina's superstar Lionel Messi quiet and the game at 0-0 went to extra time. German striker Mario Götze provided the moment of brilliance needed to win the match. He trapped Andre Schurrle's pass with his chest and swept a wonderful left-footed volley into the net. Germany won 1-0 and were champions once again.

German striker Mario Goetze scores the only goal of the game in the 2014 World Cup semi-final against Argentina.

AGAINST THE ODDS

Here are a few teams that have produced some of the World Cup's biggest shocks...

CAMEROON 1990

The first African team to make a real World Cup impact, Cameroon produced a huge shock in their first group match by beating world champions Argentina 1–0, thanks to a goal from François Omam-Biyik. In their second game they defeated Romania 2–1 with two Roger Milla goals and topped their group. In the knockout match another two extra-time goals from striker Milla saw the men in green beat Colombia 2–1. Veteran Milla delighted the world with his goal celebrations as he danced at the corner flag. In the quarter-final Cameroon took a 2–1 lead against England through Eugène Ekeke, but lost 3–2 in extra-time through two penalties scored by Gary Lineker.

Roger Milla became a World Cup hero with his goals for Cameroon.

Croatia's first ever World Cup campaign was exciting and memorable.

CROATIA 1998

Only recognised as a country in 1992 following the Croatian War of Independence, Croatia finished third in the 1998 World Cup. The side boasted fine players such as Davor Šuker, Igor Stimac, Slaven Bilić, Robert Jarni, Zvonimir Boban and Mario Stanić. They beat Romania in the knockout round, but the highlight of the tournament came with a 3–0 quarter-final thrashing of Germany with goals from Jarni, Vlaović and Šuker. Croatia took the lead in the semi-final through a typically fine finish from Šuker, but were beaten by two goals from France's Thuram. In the third-place match Croatia defeated a strong Netherlands side 2–1.

SOUTH KOREA 2002

Joint hosts South Korea proved Asian football was on the rise by reaching the World Cup semi-final in 2006. Cleverly organised by Dutchman Gus Hiddink, the side was inspired by brilliant support from its red-shirted fans. In the knockout round Italy took the lead, but South Korea levelled two minutes from time through Seol Ki-Hyeon. In extra-time Ahn Jung-Hwan touched home the golden goal that sent the home crowd into ecstasy. Even better was to follow, with the Koreans defeating Spain 5–3 on penalties in the quarter-final to become the first Asian side ever to reach the semi-finals. The side fought hard in the semi-final against Germany, but were ultimately beaten by Michael Ballack's late goal.

South Korea's players run to celebrate reaching the World Cup semi-final – the first time an Asian team has achieved this.

WORLD CUP

1. **Who scored the winning goal in the 1974 World Cup final?**
   a) Johan Cruyff
   b) Gerd Müller
   c) Paul Breitner

2. **Who was the captain of England who received the World Cup trophy in 1966?**
   a) Bobby Charlton
   b) Geoff Hurst
   c) Bobby Moore

3. **Which striker broke the all-time World Cup goalscoring record with 16 goals?**
   a) Miroslav Klose
   b) Thierry Henry
   c) David Villa

4. **What did Andrés Iniesta do after scoring the winning goal for Spain in the 2010 World Cup final?**
   a) Remove his shirt
   b) Kiss the turf
   c) Perform a double somersault

5. **Who was the Italian player headbutted in the chest by Zinedine Zidane in the 2006 World Cup final?**
   a) Andrea Pirlo
   b) Gianluigi Buffon
   c) Marco Materazzi

6. **Who was the manager of England's 1966 World Cup winning side?**
   a) Bobby Robson
   b) Walter Winterbottom
   c) Alf Ramsey

7. **With what part of his body did Diego Maradona score his first goal against England in the 1986 World Cup?**
   a) Hand of God
   b) Head of Diego
   c) Knee of Argentina

8. **What was the name of Spain's passing style at the 2010 World Cup?**
   a) Ticker tape
   b) Tick tock
   c) Tiki taka

9. **Who scored Brazil's fourth goal in the 1970 World Cup Final, often said to be the greatest team goal of any World Cup?**
   a) Pelé
   b) Carlos Alberto
   c) Jairzinho

10. **What side did Italy beat with two goals in two minutes of the semi-final of the 2006 World Cup?**
    a) Brazil
    b) Spain
    c) Germany

11. **What term referred to the Netherlands' style of play at the 1974 World Cup?**
    a) Total rubbish
    b) Total football
    c) Total brilliance

EXPERT QUIZ

12. Who scored France's third goal in the 1998 World Cup final victory against Brazil in 1998?
- **a)** Zinedine Zidane
- **b)** Marcel Desailly
- **c)** Emmanuel Petit

13. Who was the goalkeeper captain who lifted the 2010 World Cup for Spain?
- **a)** Iker Casillas
- **b)** Victor Valdes
- **c)** Pepe Reina

14. What side did Pelé score a hat-trick against in the 1958 World Cup semi-final?
- **a)** France
- **b)** Sweden
- **c)** West Germany

15. Geoff Hurst scored a hat-trick in the 1966 World Cup Final for England. But who scored England's other goal?
- **a)** Alan Ball
- **b)** Bobby Charlton
- **c)** Martin Peters

16. The 1974 Netherlands side played in what colour shirts?
- **a)** Gold
- **b)** Orange
- **c)** Yellow

17. Where in South Africa was the 2010 World Cup final played?
- **a)** Johannesburg
- **b)** Cape Town
- **c)** Durban

18. Who scored the winning goal in the 2014 World Cup final for Germany?
- **a)** Thomas Müller
- **b)** Mario Götze
- **c)** Toni Kroos

19. Who was captain of West Germany's victorious 1974 side?
- **a)** Franz Beckenbauer
- **b)** Sepp Maier
- **c)** Berti Vogts

20. Which Brazil player scored in every match of the 1970 World Cup?
- **a)** Pelé
- **b)** Rivelino
- **c)** Jairzinho

Answers: 1)b 2)c 3)a 4)a 5)c 6)c 7)a 8)c 9)b 10)c 11)b 12)c 13)a 14)a 15)c 16)b 17)a 18)b 19)a 20)c

GLOSSARY

4-4-2 formation: A football team formation made up of four defenders, four midfielders and two strikers.

Adversity: Hardship. A difficult period of time when things are not going well for a team.

Centre forward: The main striker, often a bigger player in the middle of the front line.

Character: Teams are said to show character when they overcome a series of setbacks to gain something from a game.

Chest trap: Controlling the ball on your chest.

Concede: To let in a goal.

Cruyff turn: A move made popular by Johan Cruyff in 1974. It involves a dummy and drag back of the ball that deceives a defender.

Extra-time: A period of 30 extra minutes that is played if a knockout game is a draw at the end of the standard 90 minutes.

Free kick: Awarded when a player is fouled. The fouled team is given a free kick at the ball with no opposition player allowed within ten yards (9.1 metres) of them.

Golden goal: A rule, later abandoned, where the first team to score in extra-time then wins the match.

Handball: When a player controls the ball with his hand.

Hat-trick: When a player scores three goals.

Injury-time: The time added on by the referee after the standard 90 minutes are finished.

Lap of honour: When the winning team run around the pitch to celebrate a win with their fans

Man-mark: When a defender closely follows an attacker wherever he goes.

Playmaker: A midfield player who can create chances against a defence through the use of clever passes and dribbling skill.

Relegate: To go down a level or division.

Samba football: Samba is a type of music and dance that is popular in Brazil. Samba football describes to the skilful, joyful style of Brazilian football.

Shot-stopper: A goalkeeper capable of fine saves is referred to as a shot-stopper.

Tactics: The formations and changes of players that managers use to try to win games.

Tiki taka: The short-passing style of play made famous by the Spanish football team.

Total football: A fluid style of play created by the Netherlands side of 1974 involving players skilful enough to swap positions.

Veteran: An older player approaching retirement. A veteran in football usually describes a player older than 30.

WORLD CUP WINNERS TABLE

Year	Winners	Final score	Runners-up	Venue	Location
1930	Uruguay	4-2	Argentina	Estadio Centenario	Montevideo, Uruguay
1934	Italy	2-1	Czechoslovakia	Stadio Nazionale PNF	Rome, Italy
1938	Italy	4-2	Hungary	Stade Olympique de Colombes	Paris, France
1950	Uruguay	2-1	Brazil	Estádio do Maracanã	Rio de Janeiro, Brazil
1954	West Germany	3-2	Hungary	Wankdorf Stadium	Bern, Switzerland
1958	Brazil	5-2	Sweden	Råsunda Stadium	Solna, Sweden
1962	Brazil	3-1	Czechoslovakia	Estadio Nacional	Santiago, Chile
1966	England	4-2	West Germany	Wembley Stadium	London, England
1970	Brazil	4-1	Italy	Estadio Azteca	Mexico City, Mexico
1974	West Germany	2-1	Netherlands	Olympiastadio	Munich, West Germany
1978	Argentina	3-1	Netherlands	Estadio Monumental	Buenos Aires, Argentina
1982	Italy	3-1	West Germany	Santiago Bernabéu	Madrid, Spain
1986	Argentina	3-2	West Germany	Estadio Azteca	Mexico City, Mexico
1990	West Germany	1-0	Argentina	Stadio Olimpico	Rome, Italy
1994	Brazil	0-0 (3-2 on penalties)	Italy	Rose Bowl	Pasadena, California, USA
1998	France	3-0	Brazil	Stade de France	Paris, France
2002	Brazil	2-0	Germany	International Stadium	Yokohama, Japan
2006	Italy	1-1 (5-3 on penalties)	France	Olympiastadion	Berlin, Germany
2010	Spain	1-0	Netherlands	Soccer City	Johannesburg, South Africa
2014	Germany	1-0	Argentina	Estádio do Maracanã	Rio de Janeiro, Brazil

FURTHER INFORMATION

WEB LINKS

http://www.youtube.com/watch?v=0HrjevD2vhk
Brazil's wonderful team goal (1970)

http://www.youtube.com/watch?v=U1k7DGqRF5g
The famous Cruyff turn (1974)

http://www.fifa.com/classicfootball/video/video=1083380/index.html
England win the World Cup (1966)

http://news.bbc.co.uk/sport1/hi/football/world_cup_2010/8808966.stm
Iniesta wins the World Cup for Spain (2010)

BOOKS

Foul Football: Wicked World Cup, Michael Coleman (Scholastic, 2010)
Inside Sport: World Cup Football, Clive Gifford (Wayland, 2010)
The World Cup: World Cup 2010, Michael Hurley (Heinemann, 2010)

32

25/10/17

CAERLEON

INDEX

Argentina 4, 8, 13, 16–17, 25, 26
Australia 14, 15, 21
Austria 7

Barthez, Fabien 18, 19
Belgium 16
Bocanegra, Carlos 20
Brazil 4, 6–7, 10–11, 12, 13, 18, 19, 25
Buffon, Gianluigi 20, 21
Bulgaria 12, 16
Burruchaga, Jorge 17

Cameroon 24
Cannavaro, Fabio 20, 21
Casillas, Iker 22, 23
Chile 15
Colombia 26
Croatia 18, 27
Cruyff, Johan 12, 13, 14
Czechoslovakia 11

Denmark 18

East Germany 13, 15
England 5, 7, 8–9, 11, 16, 26

France 4, 7, 8, 18–19, 21, 25, 27

Garrincha 6, 7
Germany 20, 21, 22, 23, 24–25, 27
Götze, Mario 25

Henry, Thierry 18, 19
Honduras 5
Hungary 4
Hurst, Geoff 8, 9

Iniesta, Andrés 22, 23
Italy 4, 5, 11, 16, 18, 20–21, 27

Lahm, Philipp 25

Maradona, Diego 4, 16, 17
Mexico 8, 16
Milla, Roger 26
Moore, Bobby 8, 9

Müller, Gerd 13, 15
Müller, Thomas 25

Neeskens, Johan 12, 13
Netherlands 4, 5, 12–13, 14, 15, 23, 27

Paraguay 18, 23
Pelé 6, 7, 10, 11
Peru 11
Poland 15
Portugal 8, 23
Puyol, Carlos 22, 23

Ramsey, Sir Alf 8, 9
Rep, Johnny 12, 13
Romania 11, 26, 27

Saudi Arabia 18, 19
South Africa 18, 23
South Korea 16, 27
Soviet Union 7
Spain 4, 5, 22–23, 27
Sweden 6, 7, 13, 15
Switzerland 23

Tiki taka 22
Tostão 10, 11

Ukraine 21
Uruguay 7, 8, 11
USA 20

Vogts, Berti 14, 15

Wales 7
West Germany 4, 5, 8, 9, 13, 14–15, 17

Yugoslavia 15

Zidane, Zinedine 18, 19, 20, 21